Here's to Trying!

Gracie Shields

BookLeaf Publishing

India | USA | UK

Presentation by *BookLeaf Publishing*

Web: www.bookleafpub.com

E-mail: info@bookleafpub.com

ISBN: 9789360943189

First edition 2024

To the people who have waited their entire lives to hear "It's okay, kid, here's to trying!"

Another day, another depression

I woke up this morning
with tears already welling up in my eyes.
Nightmares plagued my rest,
giving me no reprieve from my mourning.

I go to work with my face still red
and pass, numbly, through the daily motions.
Therapy never did really help anything,
so I grin and bear the thoughts in my head.

And I am aware of my constant regression.
I lose serotonin like Charlie Gordon loses IQ
points.
I, too, empathize more with a lab rat than with
my peers.
But I wake up, morning after morning.
Another day, another depression.

Puppet Show

I don't know who I am no more,
but did I ever know before?
Has my life been by my design,
or am I reading someone else's lines?
Are these my dreams? Are these my visions?
Or someone else's hopes, someone else's
ambitions?
I ask and ask, but still, I don't know,
so I read the lines and I live the show.

What happened to me?

What happened to me?
To the person I used to be?
To the girl I once was,
who always felt loved?

I know now that I'll never measure up.

The girl I used to know,
dead and buried with my hope.
There's no way, no how,
no promise, no vow.

I know now that I'll never measure up.

Wasting Time

Have you ever seen the sun
set with a mournful sigh -
as though it pains it to see
yet another Wasted Day

As you laid there, suffocating,
beneath heavy lightweight sheets
pressing you to the mattress
with The Weight of the World

Siphoning vigor, siphoning life,
filling you with shadow as light
siphons light, and it burns your soul
like Breath of Hell

The Clock

Tick-tock, the clock,
that unworthy king
around whom my life revolves.
I get no control, no control.

Meddling, meddling
where no king should.
Cut short my time with Time.

For Time, through time,
cut short my life.
Cut short my time with Time.

Ode to a Jack Pine

O jack pine, if I had thy strength -
Thine unending perseverance and
Ability to face the wind and not break

Thine ability to face the elements -
To bend with the weather and
Receive no harmful effects

Thine ability to stand tall with mirth -
To take thy scars in stride and
Know thy beauty and worth

Thy courage in the cycle of rebirth -
The first to grow from ashes and
Bring life back to the scorched earth

O then might I have the strength to face
the fires and winds that come my way

Autumn's Child

She was born to Spring, but she is Autumn's
child.
Her eyes bear the blue of a Springtime sky,
her hair the gold of a flower grown wild,
but her lips are the red of a leaf as it dries.

She takes up the rich scent of decay
and wraps it around herself like a shroud.
She was born of the season of naivete,
but the season of dying welcomes the
disavowed.

She might have been born to the sweetness of
Spring,
but it was Autumn that raised her up -
Autumn that showed her that life can sting,
and that she doesn't always need to be loved.

Just The Way You Taught Me

As a kid, I had dirt under my nails
I had tangled hair and sunburnt skin
From our many adventures

Daddy-daughter dates made me smile
Now they're a distant memory under my skin
Of when we both were younger

As a father, you taught me so much
Before your anger and pain took over your heart
And you grew more and more distant

I still wash my hair first and my body second
So that the dirt from my hair doesn't mar my
skin
Just the way you taught me as a kid

I learned all too late that in the end
You were the cause of my scarred skin
And the dirt that runs off my shoulders.

My father's daughter

I am my father's daughter -
with his sharp jaw, and angry brow.
He passed down many things to me,
namely his bottomless pit of rage
and his ability to play the victim.

I am my father's oldest child -
I comforted his sons, showed them love.
I gave them the kindness he couldn't
bring himself to publicly show.
I gave them my heart.

I am my father's least favorite child -
the one who faces his disdain,
who leans into it like a comforting hug.
For though I am my father's least favorite child,
I am the one who resembles him best.

My mother's daughter

I am my mother's daughter.
I have her eyes, and I have her heart.
I have her patience too, a blessing and a curse.
She is far too tolerant of far too much.
After all, blood is thicker than water.

I am my mother's daughter.
With all of her panic and anxiety -
the lip-picking, hair-splitting, toe-tapping
fear of all that the future may hold.
Down to my heart, I am the spit of her.

I am my mother's daughter.
I am every part of herself that she hates,
as well as every part she most admires.
So we shoulder our shared burdens,
and face each hardship with shared laughter.

The Price of Your Love

You are so much like my father
It makes me sick, but
I am doomed to follow
In my mother's footsteps

Because I would bury myself
In the ripped ground,
And tear myself to shreds
Every day for fifty years
If that should be the price of your love

Gently

I don't know how to love gently
My love is bold,
My love is strong,
My love is loud.

My love is not like the sunshine
It is not warm,
It is not soft,
It is not distant.

My love is a thunderstorm
It is unashamed,
It is powerful,
It is fierce.

If you want someone who loves
From the shadows,
From the dark,
From the silence,
You do not want my love.

Delicate

I am delicate, like a pretty glass.
Beautiful to look at,
but full of sharp edges when broken.
And you have broken me, at last.

I am delicate, like a black widow.
Petite and pretty to observe,
but deadly when your back is turned.
And yet, you gaze out the window.

I am delicate, like a bomb.
There are no "buts," no clauses.
Mishandle me and I will explode,
taking us both to our tombs.

Young Icarus

There's a certain beauty to success.
To learning, growing, taking flight.
Young Icarus, he knew this best.
To feel the sun, to feel the light.

The burning fervor of freedom,
and the other burning.
The scalding hot, hellish drips of wax.
Falling fire.

Ungrateful wretch who soared too high.
Young Icarus, he learned far too late
as he left his father, his benefactor, behind:
success means nothing in the grave.

Young Icarus, immature Icarus -
so reckless.
He wanted to be the boy who flew,
he became the boy who fell.

Fire

There's a kind of quiet thoughtfulness
That comes with fire.
As you silently sit, staring
At a force so destructive, and yet
So beautiful.

Hands clasped, mouth pressed thin.
Free and loose
Yet trapped within thought's grasp.
Eyes glazed,
The dancing tongues seen, reflected,
But not perceived.

Freedom

My heart bleeds not blood,
but words.
When I put my pen to paper
my soul pours out
onto a page of bliss,
and blood,
and agony,
and freedom.

I dream of words

17

I dream of words
of peace and pride.
Of injustices
now set aside.

Of hope, and joy,
and all that was.
Of living,
and of love.

Imaginary

Imaginary fists, paled with fright,
grip imaginary bars inside my mind.
Shackles rattle in an imaginary cell,
trapping me inside.

Imagination hidden,
by its own imaginary walls -
locked away for so long
that it can barely crawl.

Canvas

What do you say, old canvas?
Bloodred with paint, tear scarred and stained.
Tell me now, what do you say?
Of the crippling sorrow, the crippling pain
That went into the making of your scars and
stains?

What do you think, old canvas?
When you remember the life of one not so
ashamed.
Tell me now, what do you think?
Of the broken world, the broken place
That caused this hurt, this shame?

Broken Heart Bouquets

give me a world where
flowers grow from bleeding wounds
broken heart bouquets

Here's to Trying!

Here's to the kids who grew up gifted,
who set a bar for themselves,
so high they could never be expected
to actually reach it.

To the kids who joined all the clubs
Mathcounts, Debate, Battle of the Books,
not because they wanted to but
because they had to.

They felt that in some twist of fate,
they had no choice but to try
harder and harder to be great,
to push themselves.

Here's to the kids who lept over the bar,
over and over, and kept resetting it,
higher and higher, and went so far
as to vault it with a pole.

Here's to the kids who got to middle school,
and were so far ahead of the curve
that they were expected to know in full
the material that was only just being taught.

To the kids who ran as fast as they could,
but the curve caught up to them.
Faces stricken with fear as they looked
at all the people they'd disappoint.

Their parents, so used to their greatness
did not know how to praise them
for being average when they did their best,
and they expected too much.

Here's to the kids who needed a ladder
to climb their way up to the bar and prayed
that they could hold on with sweaty fingers
until they fell.

Here's to the kids who got to high school
and were so sick of learning that it seeped
into life, and their eyes became so dull
and they felt empty.

To the kids whose bodies ached
from the blow the curve delt when
it finally overtook them, and the pain
was unbearable.

They barely passed their classes,
but were still forced into advanced placement,
and they beat their heads against the glass
walls that boxed them in.

They tried to catch up, and understand,
but the burnout was immense.
They were drowning, and there was no land
to which they could swim.

Here's to the kids who grew to hate
themselves for not being good enough.
The kids who just needed to hear it's okay,
kid, here's to trying!